THE
PRAYER *of* JABEZ
for Women

STUDY GUIDE

DARLENE WILKINSON

Multnomah® Publishers *Sisters, Oregon*

THE PRAYER OF JABEZ FOR WOMEN
STUDY GUIDE
published by Multnomah Publishers, Inc.

© 2002 by Darlene Wilkinson

International Standard Book Number: 1-59052-049-1

Cover design by David Carlson Design

Cover image by Shotwell & Associates, Inc.

Scripture is from *The Holy Bible,* New King James Version (NKJV)
Copyright © 1982 by Thomas Nelson, Inc. Used by permission.

Multnomah is a trademark of Multnomah Publishers, Inc.,
and is registered in the U.S. Patent and Trademark Office.
The colophon is a trademark of Multnomah Publishers, Inc.

Printed in the United States of America

For information:
MULTNOMAH PUBLISHERS, INC.
POST OFFICE BOX 1720
SISTERS, OREGON 97759

02 03 04 05 06 07 08—10 9 8 7 6 5 4 3 2 1 0

Now Jabez was more honorable than his brothers, and his mother

called his name Jabez, saying, "Because I bore him in pain." And

Jabez called on the God of Israel saying, "Oh, that You would bless

me indeed, and enlarge my territory, that Your hand would be

with me, and that You would keep me from evil, that I may not

cause pain!" So God granted him what he requested.

1 CHRONICLES 4:9–10, NKJV

CHAPTER ONE

Made for More

1. Have you ever felt like that little girl who struggled to see the parade? What obstacles might be blocking your view of the bigger life God has in mind for you?

2. Read 1 Corinthians 2:9–16. How might having the mind of Christ help you see beyond these obstacles and give you a new perspective on what God has in store for you?

3. What does the word *honorable* mean to you? Name a woman you know whom you consider honorable. What is it about her life that impresses you? Do you consider yourself honorable? Why or why not?

4. Why do you think the Bible does not record details of Jabez's life before and after his prayer? See Romans 15:4.

5. Look up Ephesians 2:10. Do you think you are living out the unique purpose that God planned for your life before you were even born? Why or why not?

6. Look up Matthew 13:58; Mark 6:5–6; and Hebrews 11:6. What do these passages reveal about how you should pray the prayer of Jabez? Why do you think this approach is so important to God?

7. Have you ever felt God powerfully working through you to touch someone else's life for Him? What happened? How strongly do you desire to have this happen more often?

CHAPTER TWO

Invited to Ask

1. Have you ever been called a name that was negative or hurtful? What effect did it have on you? Look up 1 Peter 2:9–10. How comfortable are you describing yourself as God describes His people?

2. Jabez was given a name that disadvantaged him. Do you think there are disadvantages in your life that keep you from having a blessed life? Read Romans 8:28. How might God actually use these very things to bless you?

3. Despite his unfortunate beginning, Jabez chose to believe that God would bless him. On a scale of one to ten, how much do you believe that God *wants* to bless you and that His nature is to bless? Explain your answer.

4. Does saying "bless me" feel selfish to you? Read Matthew 7:7–8. What does this tell you about God's desire to bless and His perspective on your request?

5. Describe a time in recent days when you felt blessed by God. How did you respond? How might God's blessing to you result in His being glorified? See Luke 8:39.

6. Can you remember a time when God blessed you so that you might bless someone else? Describe how you felt.

7. How much do you trust God to know how best to bless you? Describe what you think your life might look like if God reached down to bless you—and bless you *a lot*. Is there anything still stopping you from asking for God's blessing?

CHAPTER THREE

A Life without Limits

1. If you didn't outline your territory when you first read this chapter, do so now. Are you satisfied with its size? When you think of your territory in terms of your potential to influence others for Christ, how does it change the way you feel?

2. Name two or more people upon whom you have an impact but haven't consciously tried to influence for God. What could you do this week to change that? What verses come to mind that might help motivate you?

3. Name specific areas in which we as women can become extremely busy. How might God allow us to do more for Him in each of these areas without it being "more to do"?

4. Consider the three ways (outlined in this chapter) that God might choose to answer your cry for more. Give an example of how each of these might play out in your own life. Does this prospect fill you with joyful anticipation? If not, why?

5. Write down three of your gifts or talents—things you do well—that God could use to encourage or help another person. What does Galatians 6:9–10 tell us to do and not to do?

6. Have you ever had an encounter that, looking back now, could be considered a Jabez Appointment? Describe what happened. How eager are you to experience more of these kinds of divine appointments?

7. What is the biggest dream you've had for your career or your ministry to others? How might praying the prayer of Jabez help this dream come true? What does 2 Corinthians 9:8 reveal about what God can accomplish for us?

CHAPTER FOUR

When God Steps In

1. Read 2 Corinthians 12:7–10. After Paul pleaded with the Lord, what became his response to his own situation? Discuss the different ways that we respond when we are overwhelmed or convinced that God's hand on us is not enough. How can we come to have the same response Paul had—and genuinely mean it?

2. Describe a time when you knew that God's hand was on you in a frightening or overwhelming situation. What happened? What convinced you that God was at work?

3. Look at Jesus' response in Matthew 26:39. Why is it sometimes difficult to depend completely on God? Name some of the fears that we face when we depend upon God's hand to provide for us. What does 2 Timothy 1:7 tell us?

4. According to Galatians 5:22–25, how is God's hand evidenced in our lives? How does the statement of Jesus in Mark 10:27 convince us that God's hand on us will make a difference?

5. Read Acts 4:19–31. How did God's hand provide for Peter and John? Discuss the differences between the presence and the absence of God's hand in the following situations: in a ministry opportunity, in parenting, in marriage, and in the marketplace.

6. What did Queen Esther do before seeing God's hand provide for her? (See Esther 4:15–16.) How might prayer and fasting help us to experience God's hand on us? (See Nehemiah 1:4–6.)

7. Have you found that it's harder to lean on God in areas where you do have certain skills, talents, and strengths? How could you become intentionally dependent on God when you least feel the need for His help?

CHAPTER FIVE

Safe *to* Succeed

1. In our culture, what would the average person consider to be "evil"? As a Christian, how would you define the word *evil*?

2. What did God say to Moses in Leviticus 10:3? When we regard God as holy, how does it change our perspective on evil?

3. Why does Satan seek to devour (1 Peter 5:8) those who want to do more for God and who depend upon God's Spirit to accomplish His purposes? What encouragement does James 4:7 give us?

4. Together, look over the list of temptations women face (found in this chapter). Which of these do you

identify with most? What steps can you take to avoid temptation? Share helpful tips with one another. See Ephesians 4:26–32 for some practical advice.

5. When we pray "keep me from evil," we are asking not only to be kept from the act of sinning, but also to be protected from any evil that might be inflicted upon us. How might we take steps to protect our homes and families from outside evil influences? What does God promise us in 2 Thessalonians 3:2–3?

6. How have you experienced the pain that your sin causes? How have you experienced the pain that other people's sin causes?

7. What wonderful promise did John give us in 1 John 1:9? How might practicing this truth aid the flow of God's blessing into our lives?

CHAPTER SIX

Never the Same

1. How has learning about the prayer of Jabez changed your view of what God wants for your life? How does it change the way you think about your future?

2. Read what Jesus said in John 10:10. How would you describe a person who has a "more abundant" life? Is this how you would describe your own life? Why or why not?

3. How could you develop a Jabez lifestyle? What changes might that involve for you personally?

4. How regularly will you commit to pray the prayer of Jabez in the coming months? How do you think this commitment will affect the rest of your prayer life?

5. Discuss how a woman who has been praying the prayer of Jabez for many years might describe her life, versus a woman who hasn't. What might be different about these women, their families, their character qualities, and their faith?

6. Read Colossians 4:2–6. How does this passage echo the requests in Jabez's prayer?

7. At the end of your life, if you could write a three-sentence summary of all that you became and did for God in your lifetime, what would you want it to say?

The publisher and author would love
to hear your comments about this book.

PLEASE CONTACT US AT:

www.multnomah.net/theprayerofjabez